21 Poems For Children

Miriam Babooram

BookLeaf
Publishing

India | USA | UK

Presentation by *BookLeaf Publishing*

Web: www.bookleafpub.com

E-mail: info@bookleafpub.com

ISBN: 9789360942885

First edition 2024

DEDICATION

To my incredible nieces Ophelia, Esmé, Aria and Renée.

You are the best nieces in the world.

Thank-you for inspiring me.

ACKNOWLEDGEMENT

I would like to thank my wonderful nieces, Ophelia, Esmé, Aria and Renée, without your ideas and inspiration I would never have been able to write this book of poems. I loved hearing all you ideas and I hope I've done a good job of making them come alive.

I would also like to thank my incredible sister-in-law Laura, for your enthusiasm for this book and for giving me ideas and encouragement too.

To my brother, Davey, thank-you for your ideas and your strength.

To my sister Samantha, who was the first person to hear all my poems and my-dum-di-dums, thank-you for your patience.

And to my Mam, Sally, who, whenever I was bored as a child would tell me to go and write a poem or a story, thank-you for giving me the gift of creating other worlds and places.

So this is for you, my family, I love you with all my heart.

PREFACE

The challenge was to write twenty one poems in twenty one days.

I decided to write a book of children's poetry and asked my nieces for inspiration. They gave me titles and ideas and I wrote some fun poems because of their wonderful imagination.

Fred, The Monster Under My Bed

At night when I go to bed,
I close my eyes and nod my head,
And just as slumber is about to call,
I hear an almighty roar,
from under my bed!
It's that annoying monster Fred.
He won't let me sleep, he wants to play,
But I've been awake all day.
"Fred, just let me sleep"
He pushes my nose "Beep! Beep!"
He jumps on my bed, jumps up and down.
"Fred, please stop messing around."
He throws all my clothes all over the floor.
Then he tries to slam my door.
"Fred, you'll wake up Mam and Dad"
That would be really bad.
He swings on my lampshade and shouts
"Weeeeee!"
"Fred! Look what you are doing to me.
I am really not impressed,
Look at all this mess.
What am I supposed to do,
I am so disappointed in you."
"Sorry" he says and blows his nose,

And starts to pick up all my clothes.
I help him to put them back in the drawer
After all what are friends for,
And it's not Fred's fault he wanted to play,
He hasn't seen me all day.
He's just a little monster, who likes to have fun.
And after all the tidying is done,
We tell each other stories till Fred starts to snore,
And gently Fred falls down onto the floor,
He's rolls back under my bed,
And quietly says,
"Goodnight."

The Bubble Gum Bubble

Ophelia is very good,
At blowing bubble gum,
She waits till all the flavour's gone,
Then wraps in round her tongue.

She takes an enormous breath,
In through her nose,
And then...

She blows.
And the bubble grows,

She blows.
And the bubble grows,

She blows.
And the bubble grows.

The bubble starts of
The size of a mouse,
But pretty soon
It's the size of a house!

Then a gust of wind,
Takes the bubble into the sky,

With Ophelia attached!
She's going so high.

Up through the clouds,
She can't stop.
She holds on with her teeth,
Prays the bubble won't pop.

A bird lands on the bubble,
And bounces around,
Along come it's friends,
They weigh the balloon down.

And slowly Ophelia,
Heads to the floor,
But a bird pecks the bubble,
She's not going slow any more!

The bubble has burst.
She is whizzing around.
She holds on tight
As it zips to the ground.

She lands with a crash!
Bubble gum everywhere,
Stuck to her face,
Her knees and her hair.

Rainbow the Unicorn (who has wings and likes cucumber sandwiches)

A unicorn invited me to tea one day.
She said "Aria, do you want to come and play?"
And I said " Yes of course."
Everyone wants to play with a magical horse.
She said "Hop on my back and we'll fly up
high."
And we flew through all the fluffy clouds in the
sky.
The sun was shining warm and hot,
Then all of a sudden there was a big Splosh.
We felt the rain splash against our backs,
We heard the thunder, saw the lightning crack.
I held on tight to the unicorn's mane.
"Don't worry." she said, "Rainbow is my name."
"Rain and sunshine go perfectly together,"
"Let's fly up higher, this is my favourite
weather."
The unicorn flew quickly through the storm,
She found a cloud to sit on all snuggly and
warm.
"We can watch the weather from here." she said,

"And I've made us some sandwiches with
colourful bread."
I had a bite of the sandwich, it tasted delicious,
It tasted like cucumber, my dreams and my
wishes.
I snuggled beneath her wings made of feathers,
We quietly ate cucumber sandwiches together.
Then all of a sudden a rainbow shone through,
The unicorn whispered "That's especially for
you."
I smiled at the rainbow, it's the prettiest thing.
It's all the same colours as the unicorn's wings.
Then slowly the rainbow faded away,
I've had the most magical, wonderful day.

Fussy Eater

On Monday, I will only eat chicken nuggets, that
is all.
On Tuesday, I don't want chicken nuggets at all.
On Wednesday, all my food needs to be in
straight lines,
On Thursday, the messiest plate is all mine.
On Friday, I won't eat anything green.
On Saturday, only food that starts with an E.
On Sunday I will eat all of my food.
Mum says I am fussy, that's a bit rude!

Before 7am

Thirty seconds of peace and quite,
Before it all begins,
I've prepped four different breakfasts,
And it's not even 7am.

I've ironed all the uniforms,
Fixed the stitching on a hem,
I've found four pairs of matching socks,
And it's not even 7am.

I've made all the packed lunches,
Some with cheese and some with ham,
One juice box has exploded,
And it's not even 7am.

I've scrubbed clean the toilet,
And I've emptied out the bins,
I've put on a load of washing,
And it's not even 7am.

And soon the alarms will start beeping,
They'll all be shouting "Mam!"
But I've got thirty seconds of quiet,
Just before it's 7am.

Fancy Giraffe

There was a giraffe,
With a twirly moustache,
A tiny top hat,
And a bright red cravat.

A most beautiful smile,
His neck as long as a mile.
I've known him a while,
He's got impeccable style.

HAPPY

Things that make me happy:

H - hippos, hiccups, hula hoops, hot sunny days.

A - angels, avocados, aliens, any type of chocolate,

P - pandas, puddles, pomegranates, peas.(That's a joke, no-one likes peas.)

P - planes, piglets, paint, plants.

Y - yellow, yogurt, yo-yos, you.

I Love Baa Baa

Renée had a little lamb,
And he would always bleat,
So she called him Baa Baa,
He really was quite sweet.

Everywhere that Renée went,
He trotted right behind,
She fed him grass and biscuits,
She really was quite kind.

She took Baa Baa to school one day,
It was the best thing ever.
Baa Baa and Renée have so much fun,
When they are together.

Annoying Little Sister

My little sister follows me,
She's like a little shadow.
(Like a little shadow.)

Everywhere that I go,
She will always follow.
(Will always follow.)

She copies everything I say
(Thing I say)
She copies me every day.
(Every day)
It really is annoying.
(It really is annoy -)

Stop it!!

The Amazing Auntie

When my auntie comes to tea,
I love it!
We build a rocket,
And go into space!
It's an amazing place.
We blast off to the moon,
And soon,
We are bouncing around in weightlessness.

Next time she visits,
We become wizards,
And do magic.
She turns me into a frog!
I sit happily on a log,
And croak.
Then I tell a joke,
And we laugh till our tummies hurt.

We've travelled on Unicorns,
Fought dragons with swords,
And met the biggest, most dangerous, scary
dinosaurs.

My auntie is the very best.
I wonder what adventure we'll go on next.

Grand-Père's Stories

My Grand-Père's from Mauritius,
It's an island in the sea,
When he tells us all his stories,
It sounds like paradise to me.

He tells me that the sand is,
Seven different colours,
In a place called Chamarel,
He played there with his brothers.

He tells me of the dodo,
A most peculiar bird,
But it doesn't exist any more,
I find that quite absurd.

He tells me how he used to climb,
The long, tall coconut trees,
And how he'd drink the coconut milk,
And eat coconuts for tea.

He tells me how he used to play,
Amongst the sugar cane.
And how he used to chew the sugar,
As he walked down dusty lanes.

He tells me about fresh mangoes,
Such a delicious flavour,
He tells me that they dance all night,
To music they call sega.

He tells me the turtles are so big,
That you can sit upon them,
He tells me he rode one to school,
I don't know if I believe him.

I listen to Grand-Père's stories,
Every single day.
It must have been really hard,
To move so far away.

Bed Time

I don't think I'm going to bed tonight,
I think that I might,
Watch T.V. with Dad,
It's not that I'm being bad,
I just don't want to sleep.

Send me to bed,
I'll just come back down,
And start acting like a clown.
You know that it's true,
It's just what I do.

If you read me a story,
I'll stay wide awake,
Switch my light off,
I'll pretend there's a snake.
Under my bed.

If you lull me to sleep,
With a sweet lullaby,
I might fool you at first,
Then I'll start to cry.
I don't want to go to bed.

But if you are sleepy Dad,
Why not go upstairs,
And snuggle
in all those layers,
Of warm cosy blankets?

And I'll come tuck you in,
And give you a hug,
Make sure you're snug,
As a bug in a rug.
That would be good.

And maybe I'll just,
Lie next to you.
Close my eyes,
For a second or two.
...or three
...or four
....or just
.... a
.... few
..... more......

Candle Memories

This one reminds me,
Of long summer days,
Of lying in grass.
How I love to sunbathe.

This one's a sweet shop,
The smell of burnt sugar,
Choosing my favourites,
Sharing them with my brother.

This one takes me to the beach,
I long for holidays,
The spray of sea salt on my skin,
Letting my cares drift away.

Rain against my window pane,
This one makes me remember,
The flash of a lightning bolt,
And the rumble of the thunder.

This one is toasted marshmallows,
And bonfire night
The sky full of colours,
Such a beautiful sight.

When I smell this candle,
It reminds me of my home,
The fun, joy and laughter.
I know I am never alone.

Oww! Ergh! Eww!

Oww!
That's my Dad,
Coming through the door.
He stood on my Lego,
That's all over the floor.

Ergh!
That's my Mam,
Coming down the stairs,
She thought she saw a spider,
But it's just a ball of my hair.

Eww!
That's my brother,
He's in the loo,
I didn't flush the toilet,
When I had a poo!

The Worst Part of the Day
(Part 1)

Getting in the car to go to school,
I do not like it one bit
I wonder if there's a way to fool,
My Mam into thinking I am sick.

I put my shoes on very slowly,
I pretend I can only find the one,
I really can't go to school now,
If one of my shoes has actually gone.

I don't want to put my coat on,
I pretend there's a spider in my pocket,
I scream and cry and scream again,
My Mam gets me another coat out of the closet.

I drag my bag along the floor,
I think of escaping, perhaps I'll run,
But it's too late I'm at the car door,
I don't want to go to school, it's not fun.

I just stand there looking at the car,
If I get in I know that's the end,
What's happening? I'm being picked up.
I kick and I shout and I refuse to bend.

But I'm in the car now, seat buckled in,
I'm going to school, the day finally begins.

The Worst Part of the Day
(Part 2)

Getting in the car to go to school,
I do not like it one bit,
I wonder if there's a way to fool,
The kids into thinking we're going on a trip.

Why do they put their shoes on so slowly?
Don't they know we're going to be late?
They've lost one of their shoes. Oh heck.
I can't be the last parent at the school gate.

What's all the fuss? What's going on?
A spider in your pocket, well, that's new.
"Here. Take this coat out of the cupboard.
Put it on now. It's your favourite colour, blue."

"Stop dragging your bag along the floor,"
I can't wait till this nightmare is done.
And finally, they're at the car door.
Let's get to school now, this isn't fun.

"Can you just get in the car please?
I'm going to count to ten.
If I have to come round there and pick you up...
Right then. Finally you're in"

We're all in the car now, seat buckled in.
We're going to school, the day finally begins.

Quavers

Quavers are my favourite crisps.
The cheesy taste on my tongue,
Reminds me of the school playground,
The fun I had when I was young.

I would play tag for hours,
Running for my life,
I'd swing on the monkey bars,
And speed down the slide.

It would be freezing out,
But I didn't mind,
I had dragon's breath.
There'd be adventure to find.

I'd laugh and I'd giggle,
with all of my friends,
and we'd always be sad,
when play time would end.

I am thirteen years old now,
Break times aren't the same,
I've no time for eating quavers,
Or playing silly school games.

Toothbrush

You can't talk with a toothbrush in your mouth,
Well, you can but it would be quite messy.
Instead just move the tooth brush round and round.
And let your mouth get minty freshy.

Nanna's Knitting

Nanna is always knitting,
Her needles go clickety-click,
In just a few short minutes,
She's knitted a bright yellow mit.

A few moments more,
Her needles clickety-clack,
She's knitted a duck,
That waddles and quacks.

She just keeps on knitting,
Her needles are quick,
She's knitted a family,
Of soft fluffy chicks.

Her needles are fast,
She just keeps on going,
She's knitted a garden,
and it won't stop growing.

Her knitting is rapid,
She makes so much stuff,
But she just loves knitting,
There's never enough.

She'll never stop knitting,
It's all that she does.
Her house is so full,
Of the things that she loves.

Dinosaur Adventures

Esmé once got captured,
By a Tyrannosaurus Rex,
She was playing in the garden,
And he jumped over the fence.

He picked her up with his little arms,
And threw her in a sack,
He gave a great big mighty ROAR,
Flung the sack onto his back.

Then he ran really fast,
Back to his dino cave.
He let Esmé out of the sack,
And gave her a little wave.

Even though she was a little scared,
She followed the T-Rex,
They went deeper into the cave,
You won't believe what happened next.

Esmé's eyes grew wide with wonder,
She saw so many dinosaurs,
A stegosaurus and a diplodocus,
Were laughing and eating s'mores.

The pterodactyls flew around,
Velocirapers were racing,
The brontosaurus hula hooped,
The tricerotops was dancing.

Esmé joined the party,
She slide down the Diplodocus' neck,
She hula-ed with the brontosaurus,
She roared with the T-Rex.

Esmé was having so much fun,
With all the dinosaurs.
She was learning how to,
Do all their different roars.

But then Esmé had to go,
She roared her last goodbye
T-Rex carried her back home,
Esmé wanted to cry,

She's had the best adventure,
With all the dinosaurs,
She couldn't wait to go back,
And practice all her ROARS

Back To London

I am hiding in my auntie's suitcase,
So she,
Can take me,
Back to London.

I took out all her clothes so I would fit,
So she,
Can take me,
Back to London.

I've got an orange juice and a packet of crisps,
So she,
Can take me,
Back to London.

My torch is on, it's dark in here,
So she,
Can take me,
Back to London,

I had a wee before I got in,
So she,
Can take me,
Back to London.

Oh wow! We're moving along the road!
I guess she,
Is taking me,
Back to London.